LANDMARKS of LIBERTY

Visit

MOUNT RUSHMORE

By Mary O'Mara

Gareth Stevens
Publishing

Please visit our website, www.garethstevens.com. For a free color catalog of all our high-quality books, call toll free 1-800-542-2595 or fax 1-877-542-2596.

Library of Congress Cataloging-in-Publication Data

O'Mara, Mary, 1939-
Visit Mount Rushmore / Mary O'Mara.
    p. cm. — (Landmarks of liberty)
Includes index.
ISBN 978-1-4339-6390-2 (pbk.)
ISBN 978-1-4339-6391-9 (6-pack)
ISBN 978-1-4339-6388-9 (library binding)
1. Mount Rushmore National Memorial (S.D.)—Juvenile literature. I. Title.
F657.R8O46 2012
917.83'93—dc23
                                              2011020269

First Edition

Published in 2012 by
Gareth Stevens Publishing
111 East 14th Street, Suite 349
New York, NY 10003

Copyright © 2012 Gareth Stevens Publishing

Designer: Andrea Davison-Bartolotta
Editor: Therese Shea

Photo credits: Cover, back cover (all), (pp. 2–3, 21, 22–23, 24 flag background), (pp. 4–21 corkboard background), pp. 1, 5, 6, 7 (main image), 9 (inset) Shutterstock.com; p. 7 (inset) courtesy of South Dakota State Archives; pp. 9 (main image), 17 Frederic Lewis/Getty Images; p. 11 (Washington) iStockphoto/Thinkstock; p. 11 (Jefferson, Lincoln, Roosevelt) Stock Montage/Getty Images; p. 13 Popperfoto/Getty Images; p. 14 Archive Photos/Getty Images; p. 15 FPG/Hulton Archive/Getty Images; p. 19 Fotosearch/Getty Images; p. 20 Mark Hall/Stockbyte/Getty Images.

Printed in the United States of America

CPSIA compliance information: Batch #CW12GS: For further information contact Gareth Stevens, New York, New York at 1-800-542-2595.

Contents

Words in the glossary appear in **bold** type the first time they are used in the text.

Famous Faces

Can you imagine being so important that people cut a giant likeness of your face into a mountain? Now imagine that millions of people travel great distances each year just to see it! This happened to four presidents who were especially important to the history of our country. You can see the **granite** likenesses of George Washington, Thomas Jefferson, Abraham Lincoln, and Theodore Roosevelt at the Mount Rushmore National **Memorial** in South Dakota. About 2 million people a year do!

Tell Me More!

Mount Rushmore was named after lawyer Charles E. Rushmore in the 1880s. He asked miners if the **peak** had a name. They named it after him!

4

Although visitors can't climb on the memorial to see the likenesses up close, there are plenty of beautiful views from below.

The Father of Mount Rushmore

Mount Rushmore is famous today, but have you ever wondered how it got there? It wouldn't have happened without one man—Doane Robinson. He was the state **historian** of South Dakota. He wanted more Americans to visit his state.

In the western part of South Dakota are beautiful mountains called the Black Hills. Robinson thought a **carving** in these mountains might bring visitors. The carving had to be special, so the people who carved it had to be very talented.

The Black Hills got their name from the Lakota Indians. The tree-covered hills look very dark from far away.

Doane Robinson

7

The Sculptor

In 1924, Doane Robinson wrote to **sculptor** Gutzon Borglum. Borglum had been working on a carving of **Confederate** general Robert E. Lee on Georgia's Stone Mountain. It was said to have looked so much like the general that it made Lee's soldiers cry for their beloved leader.

Borglum visited Robinson in South Dakota in 1924 and 1925. During the second visit, he saw Mount Rushmore, a peak that rose above the surrounding Black Hills. This was the location he chose for the carving.

Tell Me More!

Robinson's first ideas for the carving were likenesses of Sioux chief Red Cloud, explorers Meriwether Lewis and William Clark, and Buffalo Bill Cody, who was famous for his Wild West shows.

Gutzon Borglum didn't just plan the carving, he did much of the work. Here, he works below the eye of Abraham Lincoln.

GUTZON BORGLUM

Sculpted by his son
Lincoln Borglum

Why These Presidents?

The US presidents shown on Mount Rushmore were chosen carefully. George Washington was the general who led the American colonial army against England. As the first US president, he set an example for those who followed. Thomas Jefferson wrote the Declaration of Independence. As president, he doubled the country's size with the **Louisiana Purchase**. Abraham Lincoln kept the nation from falling apart throughout the Civil War and helped end slavery. Theodore Roosevelt helped US trade through the building of the **Panama Canal**. He also fought for workers' rights.

Tell Me More!

Gutzon Borglum was the first to suggest carving George Washington and Abraham Lincoln. Thomas Jefferson and Theodore Roosevelt were decided upon later.

George Washington

Thomas Jefferson

Abraham Lincoln

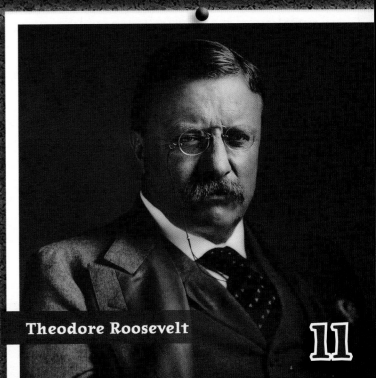

Theodore Roosevelt

11

Hanging at Work

On October 4, 1927, work began on Mount Rushmore. Each morning, workers climbed to the top of the mountain on a stairway of 506 steps. A small railroad called a tramway was built to carry supplies and tools. Later, it was strengthened to carry people.

Once at the top, workers got into leather **harnesses** joined to cables. Then, they were lowered to their workplace on the face of the mountain by a **winch**. If workers needed to move, they yelled to a "call-boy" who stood between them and the workers at the winches. He passed on any messages.

Tell Me More!

About 400 workers labored on Mount Rushmore from 1927 until October 1941.

Even though the work was full of danger, no one died during the carving of Mount Rushmore.

13

Dynamite!

Gutzon Borglum made a model head of each president. Each inch of the model stood for a foot of the Mount Rushmore carving. Workers used the models to shape the mountain. They marked the granite to show where and how much rock needed to be removed to create the shape of the head.

Dynamite was used to remove most of the rock. Workers drilled holes and filled them with dynamite. Twice a day, they exploded the dynamite when the other workers were at a safe distance.

dynamite worker

This photo was taken during the first days of work on the memorial. Rock dust fills the air near blasting sites.

Drills and Hammers

After the dynamite blasts, drillers used **jackhammers** to remove more stone. This prepared the surface for the carvers. It was hard work. Each jackhammer weighed over 75 pounds (34 kg)! The granite quickly dulled the jackhammers' metal bits, or points. Workers called "steel nippers" came down on harnesses to exchange bits.

Finally, the carvers went to work. They used smaller drills and hammers to make the features of each president's face. After a day's work, carvers and other workers were covered in granite dust.

Tell Me More!

After working all day, the Mount Rushmore workers stood in front of hoses full of air to blast the rock dust off themselves.

The Mount Rushmore drillers wore masks so they wouldn't breathe in rock dust. Here, they carve the eyes of Theodore Roosevelt in 1939.

17

Almost Finished

In 1930, workers encountered a problem with the head of Thomas Jefferson. The rock they had used for the carving wouldn't support its weight. They had to blast away the uncompleted head and begin again. As each head was completed, a special celebration was held.

In 1941, Gutzon Borglum died, just a few months before work was completed. His son, Lincoln Borglum, finished the job. By October 31, 1941, the carvings were complete. Mount Rushmore wasn't quite finished yet, though.

Tell Me More!

In 1937, a bill in Congress asked that the likeness of women's rights leader Susan B. Anthony be added to Mount Rushmore. Money issues stopped the idea.

Thomas Jefferson was originally positioned on the other side of George Washington. Here, US soldiers view the memorial in 1942.

19

Recording History

Gutzon Borglum had always thought that Mount Rushmore needed a written explanation. The Hall of Records, a room cut into the granite, contains the story of Mount Rushmore and what the memorial means in Borglum's own words. It was finally completed in 1998.

Today's Mount Rushmore National Memorial offers more than the amazing sight of four beloved presidents. There are walking trails, Borglum's sculpting studio, and a visitors' center. Visit Mount Rushmore yourself to understand what a true work of art it is.

Timeline of Mount Rushmore

1924 Doane Robinson writes to Gutzon Borglum asking him to create a carving in South Dakota.

1927 Work on Mount Rushmore begins.

1930 Thomas Jefferson's head is blasted and started over.

1941 The Mount Rushmore carvings are completed.

1998 The Hall of Records is completed.

Glossary

carving: an object formed by cutting and shaping a material such as stone

Confederate: having to do with the Confederate States of America during the American Civil War

dynamite: a powerful explosive

granite: a kind of rough, very hard rock often used for building

harness: a set of straps fitted to a person to keep them in place

historian: one whose job is to be knowledgeable about history

jackhammer: a handheld power tool used for splitting or drilling rock

Louisiana Purchase: territory of the western United States bought from France in 1803

memorial: something that is meant to remind people of someone who has died or an event that has happened

Panama Canal: a waterway dug across a narrow part of Panama that connects the Atlantic and the Pacific Oceans

peak: the pointed top of a mountain

sculptor: an artist who creates shapes with stone, wood, metal, or other matter

winch: a machine for lifting loads using a rope or chain that is wound by an engine or by hand

For More Information

Books

Bauer, Marion Dane. *Mount Rushmore*. New York, NY: Aladdin Paperbacks, 2007.

Riggs, Kate. *Mount Rushmore*. Mankato, MN: Creative Education, 2009.

Thomas, William David. *Mount Rushmore*. New York, NY: Chelsea Clubhouse, 2010.

Websites

Mount Rushmore National Memorial
www.nps.gov/moru/index.htm
Read all about the people and stories behind the creation of the Mount Rushmore monument.

Timeline: Mount Rushmore 1868–1999
www.pbs.org/wgbh/amex/rushmore/timeline/index.html
Learn more about how the huge project progressed year by year.

Index